The Brick Testament

Stories from the Book of Genesis

Library of Congress Cataloging in Publication Number: 2003090705

ISBN: 1-931686-45-9

Printed in Singapore

Typeset in Agincourt, Edwardian Medium, and Goudy Text MT

Designed by Andrea Leigh Stephany

Distributed in North America by Chronicle Books
85 Second Street
San Francisco, CA 94105

10 9 8 7 6 5 4 3

Quirk Books
215 Church Street
Philadelphia, PA 19106
www.quirkbooks.com

The Brick Testament
Stories from the Book of Genesis

Retold and Illustrated by Brendan Powell Smith

QUIRK BOOKS

PHILADELPHIA

Contents

Introduction

There I was enjoying a leisurely lunch one evening at the local Taco Bell when suddenly my bean burrito burst into flames and I heard the unmistakable voice of God. "Brendan," it said, "from this day forth you will illustrate for me my most holy of books, The Bible, completely in LEGO®."

"Surely there is someone more qualified than I for this task," I humbly replied. "For I am but a simple man with no special talent for building with plastic bricks."

"Who are you to question the will of God?" the angered voice boomed back. "Was it not I who created this world from nothing and whose hand controls the destiny of mankind?"

"But I'm an atheist," I protested.

"Then you are especially unqualified to question me!" came the response. "Now get to work!"

Since the day of my calling, I have labored both day and night to realize this monumental task. More than one hundred illustrated stories have been shared with the world on the phenomenally popular website, www.bricktestatment.com. Presented here for the first time in print are the first fruits of my labors: These are the stories of Genesis.

The Garden of Eden

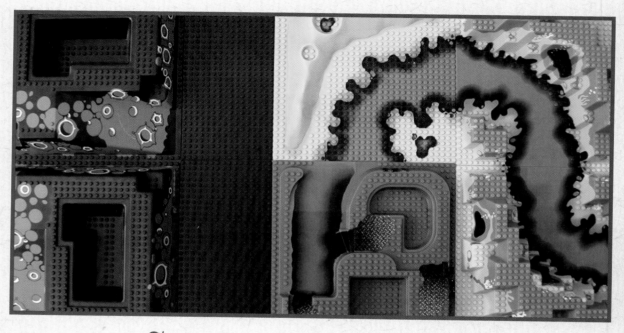

In the beginning, God created the heavens and earth.
No plant or shrub had yet sprung up, for God had not sent rain upon the earth,
and there was no one to till the soil. Moisture would well up from the earth
and water the surface of the ground.

Gn 1:1, 2:4–6

God formed man from the soil of the ground.

GN 2:7

And breathed into his nostrils the breath of life.

Gn 2:7

And man became a living creature.

Gn 2:7

God planted a garden in Eden,
and there he put the man he had formed.
God caused to sprout every tree that is
pleasing to look at and good for food,
with the tree of life in the middle
of the garden with the tree of knowledge
of good and evil.

GN 2:9

God took the man, and put him in the garden of Eden to look after and maintain it.

GN 2:15

God commanded the man, saying, "From every tree of the garden you may freely eat,
but from the tree of knowledge of good and evil, you shall not eat.
For the day that you eat from it you will surely die."

Gn 2:16–17

God said, "It is not good that the man should be alone. I shall make him a helper."

GN 2:18

From the ground God formed every animal of the field and every bird of the sky.

GN 2:19

Whatever the man called every living creature, that was its name.
The man gave names to all the cattle, every bird of the sky,
and every animal of the field. But no suitable helper was found for the man.

GN 2:19–20

Then God caused a deep sleep to fall on the man, and he slept.
He took one of his ribs, and closed up the flesh in its place.
And from the rib which God had taken from the man . . .

Gn 2:21–22

. . . he made a woman.

GN 2:22

He brought her to the man, and the man said,
"This at last is bone from my bones, and flesh from my flesh!
She will be called woman, because she was taken out of man."

Gn 2:23

And the man and his wife were both naked and not ashamed.

G<small>N</small> 2:25

Now the snake was the shrewdest of any animal of the field which God
had made. He said to the woman, "Has God really said,
'You shall not eat from any tree of the garden?'"

Gn 3:1

The woman said, "We may eat the fruit from the trees of the garden, but not the fruit from the tree in the middle of the garden. God has said, 'Do not eat from it, and do not even touch it, or else you will die.'"

Gn 3:2–3

The snake said to the woman, "Surely you will not die!
For God knows that on the day you eat from it, your eyes will be opened,
and you will be like gods, knowing good and evil."

Gn 3:4–5

The woman saw that the tree
was good for food, pleasing to the eyes,
and desirable for the knowledge it could give,
and she took fruit from it.

Gn 3:6

And ate it.

Gn 3:6

She gave some to her husband who was with her.

GN 3:6

And he ate it.

GN 3:6

The eyes of both of them
were opened,
and they knew
they were naked.

Gn 3:7

They sewed fig leaves together, and made themselves loincloths.

Gn 3:7

They heard the voice of God walking in the garden in the cool of the day,
and the man and his wife hid themselves among the trees of the garden.

Gn 3:8

God called to the man,
and said to him, "Where are you?"

Gn 3:9

The man said, "I heard your voice in the garden,
and I was afraid because I was naked,
so I hid myself."

Gn 3:10

God said, "Who told you that you were naked?
Have you eaten from the tree that I
commanded you not to eat from?"

Gn 3:11

The man said, "The woman you gave me,
she gave me fruit of the tree, and I ate it."

Gn 3:12

God said to the woman,
"What have you done?"

G<small>N</small> 3:13

The woman said,
"The snake convinced me, and I ate."

G<small>N</small> 3:13

God said to the snake,
"Because you have done this,
you are cursed above all livestock,
and above every animal of the field.
On your belly you shall go,
and you shall eat dust all the days of your life.
I will put hostility between you and the woman,
and between your offspring and hers.
They will strike your head,
and you will strike their heel."

Gn 3:14–15

To the woman he said, "I will greatly increase your suffering during childbirth. In pain you will bring forth children. Your desire will be for your husband, and he will rule over you."

Gn 3:16

To the man he said,
"You have listened to your wife,
eating from the tree about which
I commanded you, 'Do not eat from it.'
Therefore, cursed is the ground because of you.
In anguish you shall till it all the days of your life.
It will yield you thorns and thistles.
By the sweat of your face you will win your bread
until you return to the ground,
for out of it you were taken.
You are dust, and to dust you shall return.

GN 3:17–19

God made leather garments for the man and his wife, and clothed them.

GN 3:21

God said, "The man has become like one of us, knowing good and evil.
He must be prevented from reaching out his hand to take from the tree of life,
lest he eat from it and also live forever!" Therefore God sent him away
from the garden of Eden, to till the ground from which he was taken.

Gɴ 3:22–23

He drove the man away and stationed cherubs at the east of the garden of Eden, and a flaming sword which turned every way to guard the way to the tree of life.

GN 3:24

The End

Cain and Abel

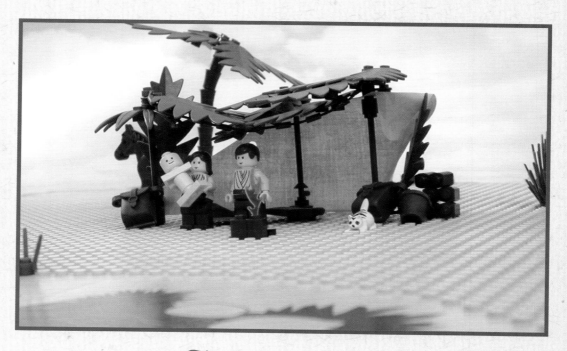

The man lay with his wife Eve.
She became pregnant and gave birth to Cain.

Gn 4:1

She gave birth again, to Cain's brother Abel.

Gn 4:2

Abel was a shepherd, and Cain was a tiller of the ground.

Gn 4:2

Cain brought God an offering from the produce of the ground,
and Abel brought the firstborn females of the flock.

Gn 4:3–4

God respected Abel and his offering.

Gn 4:4

But he did not respect Cain and his offering.
Cain became very angry, and his face was downcast.

Gn 4:5

God said to Cain, "Why are you angry? Why is your face downcast?
If you do well, is there not acceptance? If you do not do well,
sin crouches at the door. Its desire is for you, and you shall rule over it."

Gn 4:6–7

Cain said to his brother Abel, "Let's go into the field."

When they were out in the field, Cain attacked his brother Abel.

Gn 4:8

And killed him.

Gn 4:8

God said to Cain, "Where is your brother Abel?"
"I don't know," Cain replied.

GN 4:9

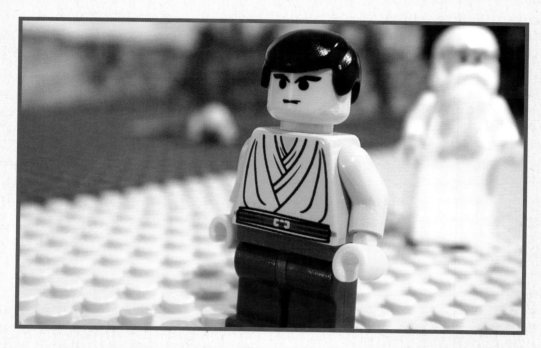

"Am I my brother's keeper?" Cain asked.
"What have you done?" said God.
"The voice of your brother's blood cries out to me from the ground."

GN 4:9–10

"Now you are cursed from the ground,
which has opened its mouth to receive
your brother's blood from your hand.
From now on, when you till the ground,
it will not yield its strength to you.
You shall be a fugitive and a
wanderer on the earth."

GN 4:11–12

Cain said to God, "My punishment is too great to endure. Today you have
driven me from the face of the land, and from your face I am hidden.
I will be a fugitive and a wanderer of the earth, and whoever finds me will kill me."

GN 4:13–14

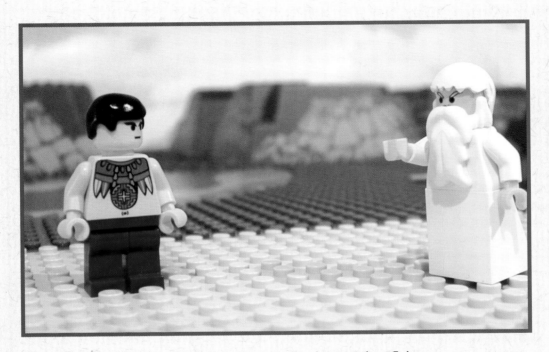

God said to him, "Very well, whoever slays Cain,
a sevenfold vengeance will be taken on him." God set a mark on Cain,
so that no one finding him would strike him down.

GN 4:15

Cain left God's presence and lived in the land of Nod, east of Eden.

Gn 4:16

The End

The Flood

The earth was corrupt before God and filled with crime.
God saw the earth, and saw that it was corrupt,
for all living beings had perverted their ways on the earth.

GN 6:11–12

God said, "I shall destroy humankind, whom I have created,
from the face of the earth—humankind, as well as animals, creeping things,
and birds of the sky. For I am sorry that I have made them."

Gn 6:7

But Noah found favor in God's eyes. God said to Noah, "The end of all living things has come, for the earth is filled with violence through them. And so I will destroy them with the earth. Make yourself an ark of gopher wood."

GN 6:8, 13–14

"Behold, I will bring a flood of waters on this earth to destroy every living thing under heaven. Everything on earth will die."

GN 6:17

Noah did everything exactly as God had commanded him.

Gn 6:22

"But I will establish my covenant with you, and you shall go into the ark—you, your sons, your wife, and your sons' wives with you. You shall bring two of every kind of living creature into the ark, a male and a female, to keep them alive with you."

Gn 6:18–19

God said to Noah, "Go into the ark with all of your household,
for I see you alone as righteous among this generation.
Of every clean animal, you shall take seven pairs."

Gn 7:1–2

"In seven days, I will cause it to rain on the earth for forty days and forty nights. Every living thing that I have made, I will destroy from the face of the earth."

Gn 7:4

Noah went into the ark with his sons, his wife, and his sons' wives, to escape the waters of the flood. After seven days, the waters of the flood came on the earth.

Gn 7:7, 10

In the six hundredth year of Noah's life, in the second month,
on the seventeenth day of the month, on the same day, all the waters under
the ground burst forth, and the sky's windows were opened.
It rained on the earth for forty days and forty nights.

GN 7:11–12

The waters greatly increased, overwhelming the earth.
And the ark floated on the surface of the waters.

GN 7:18

The waters increased even more upon the earth, so that every tall mountain under the whole of heaven was covered. And every living thing that moved on the earth died—all the birds, the livestock, the animals, and every creeping thing that creeps on the earth, and all humankind.

Gn 7:19, 21

Every last thing
with the breath of life
in its nostrils,
everything that was on
dry land,
died.

Gn 7:22

God destroyed every living thing that was on the face of the earth,
including humankind, livestock, creeping things, and birds of the sky.
They were destroyed from the earth.

GN 7:23

Then the waters receded steadily from the earth. After one hundred fifty days
the waters had decreased, so that on the seventeenth day of the
seventeenth month, the ark came to rest on the mountains of Ararat.

Gn 8:3

In the six hundred and first year of his life, Noah opened the window of the ark and looked out. He saw that the surface of the earth was dry.

Gn 8:13

Noah went out, with his sons, his wife, and his sons' wives with him.
Every animal, every creeping thing, and every bird, everything that creeps
along the earth, went out of the ark in their groups.

Noah built an altar to God, and took from every clean animal,
and of every clean bird, and sacrificed burnt offerings on the altar.

Gn 8:20

God smelled the pleasing scent, and God said to himself,
"I will never again curse the ground because of humankind,
even though the intentions of their heart are evil from youth.
Nor will I ever again destroy every living thing, as I have done."

Gn 8:21

God blessed Noah and his sons, and said to them, "Be fruitful, and multiply, and fill the earth. Be the fear and dread of every animal of the earth and every bird of the sky. Every living thing that moves will be your food, just as with plants. But you are not to eat flesh with its life in it, that is, its blood."

GN 9:1–4

"I have set my rainbow in the clouds, and it is to be a sign of the covenant between me and the earth. I will remember my covenant between me and you and every living creature. And the waters will never again become a flood to destroy all life."

Gn 9:13–15

The End

Noah's Insobriety

The sons of Noah who went out from the ark were Shem, Ham, and Japheth. Ham was the father of Canaan. These three were the sons of Noah, and from these, the whole earth was populated.

Gn 9:18–19

Noah was a farmer, and planted a vineyard.
He drank some wine and got drunk,
and was uncovered in his tent.

Gn 9:20–21

Ham, the father of Canaan,
saw his father's nakedness.

Gn 9:22

And he told his two brothers outside.

Gn 9:22

Shem and Japheth took a garment, laid it on both their shoulders,
went in backward, and covered the nakedness of their father.
Their faces were turned, and they did not see their father's nakedness.

Gn 9:23

Noah awoke from his drunkenness and knew what his youngest son had done to him, and he said, "Cursed be Canaan! He shall be his brothers' lowest slave." He went on, "Blessed of Yahweh my God be Shem, and let Canaan be his slave!"

Gn 9:24–27

Noah lived three hundred and fifty years after the flood.
Noah lived a total of nine hundred and fifty years.

<small>Gn 9:28–29</small>

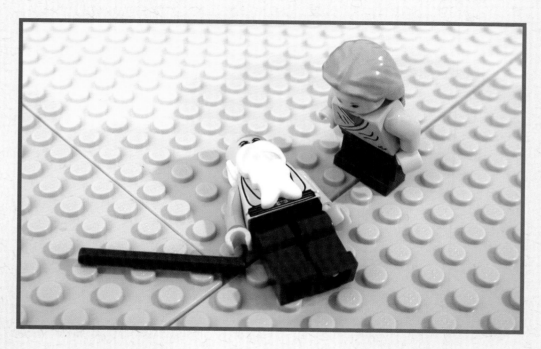

Then he died.

Gn 9:29

The End

The Tower of Babel

$\mathcal{T}$he whole earth had one language and was of one speech.
As they migrated from the east, it happened that they found a plain
in the land of Shinar, and they settled there. They said one to another,
"Come, let's make bricks, and bake them thoroughly."

Gn 11:1–3

They used bricks for stone, and asphalt for mortar. They said,
"Come, let us build ourselves a city, and a tower whose top reaches the sky.
Let us make a name for ourselves, so that we are not scattered
across the face of the earth."

Gn 11:3–4

God came down
to see the city
and the tower
that the sons
of mankind
were building.

Gn 11:5

God said, "Look! They are one people, and they all have one language,
and this is what they begin to do."

Gn 11:6

"Now nothing they plan to do will be impossible for them!"

Gn 11:6

"Come, let us go down there and confuse their language,
so that they cannot understand each other's speech."

GN 11:7

From there God scattered them abroad across the face of the earth.

GN 11:8

And they stopped building the city.

Gn 11:8

That is why it was called Babel,
because there God confused the language of all the earth.

Gn 11:9

The End

Sodom and Gomorrah

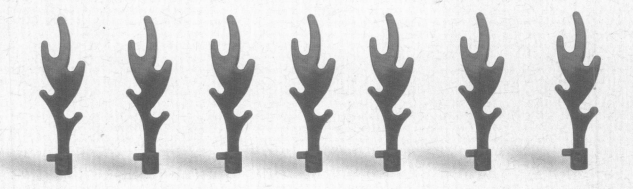

$\mathfrak{T}$wo angels came to Sodom in the evening. Lot was sitting at the gate of Sodom.

GN 19:1

"My lords," he said, "please come into your servant's house. Stay the night and wash your feet. You can wake up early, and then continue on your way."

Gn 19:2

They said,
"No, we will spend the night in the square."

G<small>N</small> 19:2

But Lot urged them greatly,
and they came in with him,
entering his house.

GN 19:3

He made them a meal and they ate.

G<small>N</small> 19:3

But before they went to bed, the men of the city of Sodom surrounded the house, both young and old, all the people from every part of the city.

GN 19:4

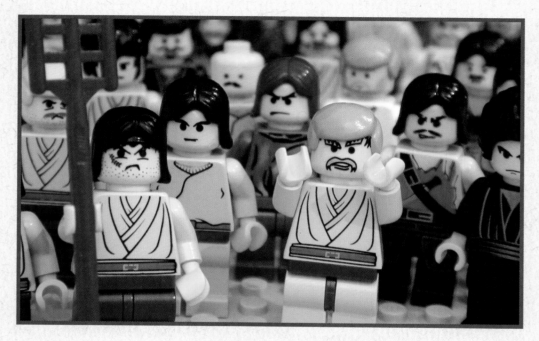

They called to Lot and said to him, "Where are the men who came to you tonight?
Bring them out to us, so that we may lie with them."

Gn 19:5

Lot went out the door and shut the door behind him.
He said, "Please, my brothers, do not be evil."

Gn 19:6–7

"Look, I have two virgin daughters. Please let me bring them out to you.
You may do whatever you please to them. Just do not do anything to these men,
for they have come under the protection of my roof."

<small>Gn 19:8</small>

"Stand back!" they said. "This one came here as a foreigner and appoints himself a judge? Now we will deal with you worse than with them!"

Gn 19:9

They pressed hard against Lot, nearly breaking down the door.
But the two men inside reached out, pulled Lot into the house, and shut the door.

Gn 19:9–10

The men said to Lot, "Do you have anybody else here?
Whoever you have in the city, take them out of here,
for we will destroy this place. God has sent us to destroy it."

GN 19:12–13

When the morning came, the angels hurried Lot, saying,
"Get up! Take your wife and your two daughters who are here,
or you will be swept away with the city's wickedness!"

Gn 19:15

But he lingered, so the men grabbed his hand and the hands of his wife
and his two daughters. They led them out and, God being merciful to them,
set them outside of the city.

Gn 19:16

When they had taken them outside, they said, "Run for your life!
Do not look behind you, and do not stay anywhere in the plain.
Flee to the mountains, or you will be destroyed!"

GN 19:17

Then God rained on Sodom and on Gomorrah
brimstone and fire from out of the sky.

Gn 19:24

He overthrew those cities, the whole plain—all the inhabitants of the cities,
and everything that grows on the ground.

Gn 19:25

Behind him, Lot's wife looked back . . .

GN 19:26

. . . and she became a pillar of salt.

Gn 19:26

The End

God Tests Abraham

It happened after these things, that God tested Abraham,
and said to him, "Abraham!"

GN 22:1

Abraham said, "Here I am."

GN 22:1

God said, "Now take your son, your only son Isaac, whom you love, and go into the land of Moriah. Sacrifice him there as a burnt offering on one of the mountains of which I will tell you."

GN 22:2

Abraham rose early in the morning and saddled his donkey.
He took two of his men with him, and Isaac his son.

GN 22:3

On the third day Abraham looked up and saw the place from afar.

Gn 22:4

Abraham said to his men, "Stay here with the donkey.
The boy and I will go over yonder and worship. We will come back to you."

Gn 22:5

Abraham took the wood for the burnt offering and laid it on Isaac his son.
He took in his hand the fire and the knife.

Gn 22:6

Isaac spoke to Abraham and said, "Father, look, here is the fire
and the wood, but where is the lamb for the burnt sacrifice?"

Gn 22:7

Abraham said, "God himself will provide the lamb for the burnt sacrifice, my son."
So they both went on together.

Gn 22:8

They came to the place which God had told him of,
and Abraham built the altar there, laying the wood in order.

Gn 22:9

He bound his son Isaac and laid him on the altar, on the wood.

Gn 22:9

Abraham reached out his hand
and took the knife to slaughter his son.

GN 22:10

But the angel of God called to him out of the sky,
and said, "Abraham, Abraham!"

GN 22:11

Abraham said, "Here I am."

GN 22:11

"Do not lay your hand on the boy or do anything to him," said the angel of God.
"For now I know that you fear God, seeing that you have not withheld your son,
your only son, from me."

GN 22:12

Then Abraham looked up and saw that behind him was a ram
caught in a thicket by his horns.

Gn 22:13

Abraham went and took the ram,
and sacrificed him for a burnt offering instead of his son.

Gɴ 22:13

The End

Jacob and His Cousins

ℒaban had two daughters.
The name of the elder was Leah, and the name of the younger was Rachel.

Gn 29:16

Leah had tender eyes.

Gɴ 29:17

But Rachel was shapely and attractive,
and Jacob fell in love with Rachel.

Gɴ 29:17–18

Jacob stayed with Laban for a month. Then Laban said to Jacob,
"Just because you are my nephew, should you be working for me for nothing?
Tell me what will your wages shall be."

GN 29:14–15

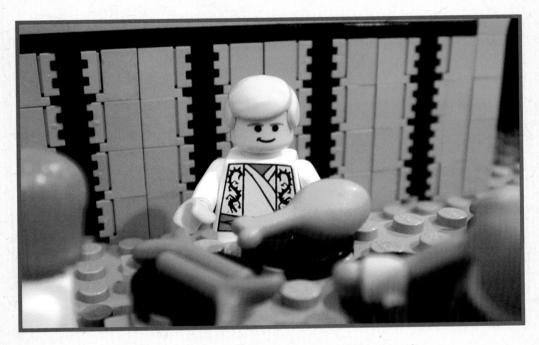

Jacob said, "I will work for you for seven years in exchange
for your younger daughter Rachel."

Gn 29:18

"It is better that I should give her to you than to some other man," said Laban. "Stay with me."

Gn 29:19

Jacob worked for seven years in exchange for Rachel.
And because of his love for her, it seemed but a few days to him.

GN 29:20

Then Jacob said to Laban, "My time is fulfilled,
now give me my wife so that I may lie with her."

Gn 29:21

Laban gathered together all the people of the area and held a wedding feast.

Gɴ 29:22

That evening, Laban took his daughter Leah and brought her to Jacob,
and he lay with her.

Gn 29:23

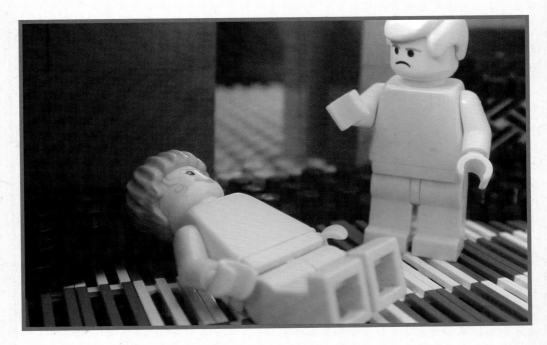

But in the morning, behold, it was Leah!

Jacob said to Laban, "What is this you have done to me?
Did I not work for you in exchange for Rachel? Why have you deceived me?"

Gn 29:25

Laban said, "It is not the local custom to marry off the younger
before the firstborn. Complete this daughter's wedding feast week, then we will give
you the other girl as well, in exchange for another seven years of work."

GN 29:26–27

Jacob did so, completing the wedding feast week, and then Laban gave him
his daughter Rachel to be his wife. And Jacob lay with Rachel as well.

Gn 29:28, 30

Jacob loved Rachel more than Leah.

GN 29:30

And he worked for Laban another seven years.

Gn 29:30

The End

Jacob Wrestles God

Jacob got up that night and sent his two wives, his two slave-girls, and his eleven children across the shallow part of the Jabbok.

Gn 32:22

Then he sent all his possessions across as well.

Gn 32:23

And Jacob was left alone.

Gn 32:24

And a man wrestled with him . . .

GN 32:24

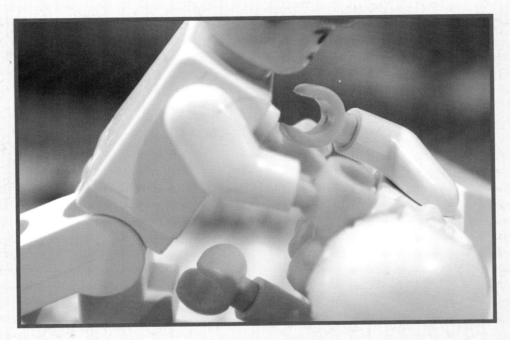

. . . until the rise of dawn.

GN 32:24

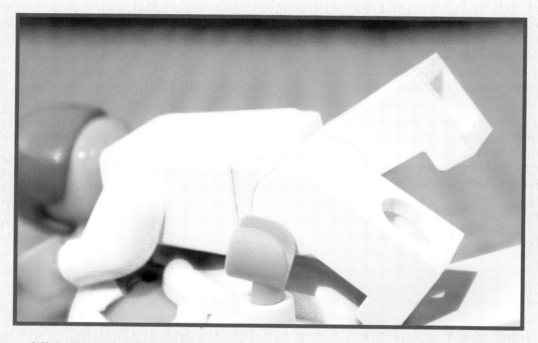

When the man saw that he could not overpower Jacob, he struck his hip socket, and Jacob's hip was dislocated as he wrestled.

Gn 32:25

The man said, "Let me go, for dawn is breaking."

Gn 32:26

Jacob said, "I will not let you go unless you bless me."

Gn 32:26

The man said to him, "What is your name?"
He said, "Jacob."

GN 32:27

The man said, "Your name will
no longer be called Jacob, but Israel,
for you have wrestled with God and with men,
and you have prevailed."

GN 32:28

Jacob asked him, "Please tell me your name."

GN 32:29

The man said, "Why do you ask my name?"

GN 32:29

And he blessed him there.

Gₙ 32:29

Jacob called the name of the place Peniel, for, he said,
"I have seen God face to face, and I am still alive."

GN 32:30

The sun rose on him as he went across Peniel, and he limped because of his hip. That is why to this day children of Israel do not eat the sinew which is attached to the socket of the hip, because the man struck the socket of Jacob's hip near the sinew.

GN 32:31–32

The End

Joseph Is Ambushed

Israel loved Joseph more than any of his other sons
because he was the son of his old age, and he made him a coat of many colors.

GN 37:3

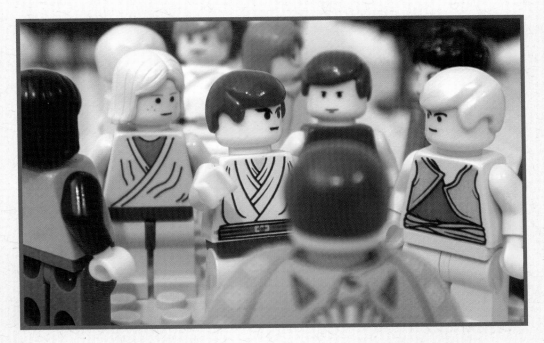

Joseph's brothers saw that their father loved him more than any of them, and they hated Joseph and could not speak a friendly word to him.

Gn 37:4

When his brothers went to graze their father's flock at Shechem,
Israel said to Joseph, "Your brothers are grazing the flock at Shechem.
Go and see if all is well with your brothers and the flock and then bring me word."

GN 37:12–14

Joseph's brothers saw him in the distance. Before he came close to them, they conspired to kill him. "Come on, let's kill him and throw him into one of the wells," they said one to another, "and we will say a wild animal has devoured him."

GN 37:18–20

"Shed no blood," Reuben said to them.
"Throw him into the well out in the desert, but lay no hand on him."

GN 37:22

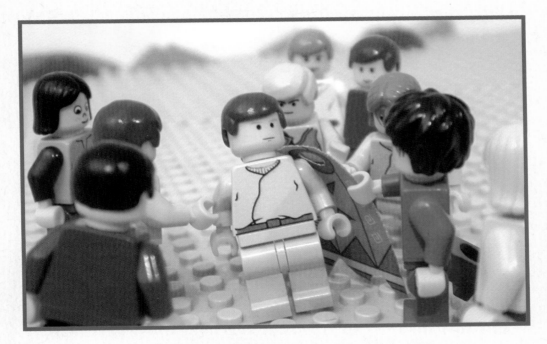

When Joseph reached his brothers, they stripped him of his coat,
the coat of many colors, which he was wearing.

Gn 37:23

They took him and threw him into the well.

GN 37:24

They took Joseph's coat, slaughtered a goat, and dipped the coat in its blood.

Gn 37:31

They sent the coat of many colors to their father, and said, "We have found this. Examine it and tell whether or not it is your son's coat."

Gn 37:32

He recognized it and said, "It is my son's coat.
A wild animal has devoured him. Joseph is surely torn to pieces."

GN 37:33

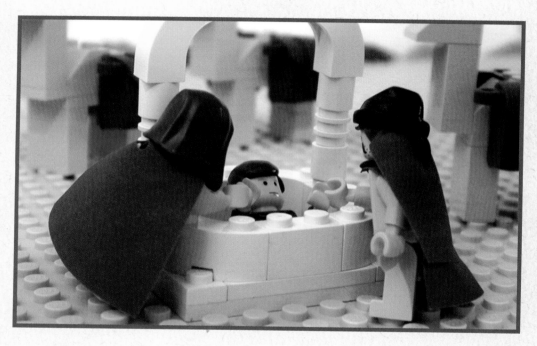

Some Midianite merchants were passing by,
and they pulled Joseph up out of the well.

GN 37:28

They sold Joseph to the Ishmaelites for twenty pieces of silver.

Gn 37:28

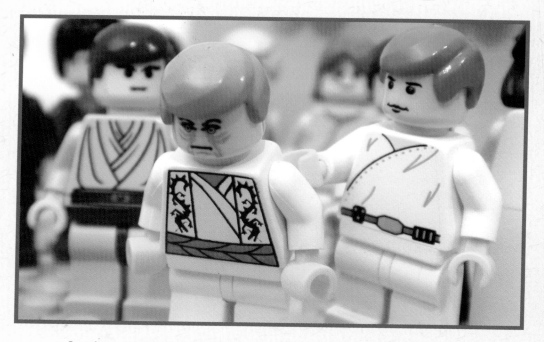

Jacob mourned for his son for many days. All his sons and daughters
tried to console him, but he refused to be consoled and said, "I will go down
to the grave mourning for my son." So Joseph's father wept for him.

Gn 37:34–35

The Ishmaelites brought Joseph to Egypt.

Gn 37:28

The End

"The Reverend" Brendan Powell Smith

About the Author

Little is known about "The Reverend" Brendan Powell Smith. His life is a mysterious enigma of puzzling paradoxes, enigmatic puzzles, and paradoxical mysteries. He keeps his public life private, and will take most of his secrets with him to the grave.

Though it remains unclear why Smith has been chosen to illustrate the Bible in LEGO®, most scholars and theologians agree it is of little use to question such matters. In near constant communication with God, "The Reverend" Brendan Powell Smith is perhaps, if not possibly, the closest thing we have to a living modern-day prophet.